The Eyes

by Susan Heinrichs Gray

MG (4-8)
ATOS 5.3
0.5 pts
Non-Fiction

89295 EN

THE EYES

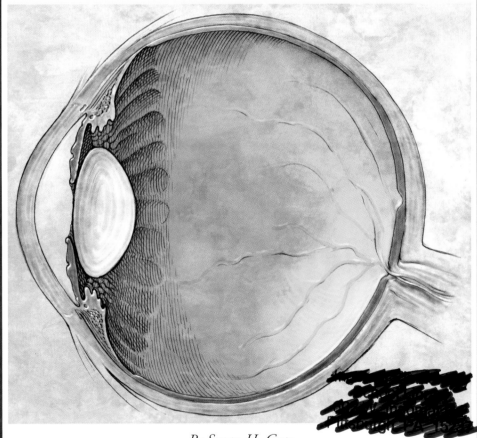

By Susan H. Gray

THE CHILD'S WORLD®
CHANHASSEN, MINNESOTA

The Child's World

Published in the United States of America by The Child's World®
PO Box 326, Chanhassen, MN 55317-0326
800-599-READ
www.childsworld.com

Content Adviser:
R. John Solaro,
PhD, Distinguished
University Professor
Head, Department
of Physiology and
Biophysics, University
of Illinois at Chicago

Photo Credits: Cover/frontispiece: Photodisc. Interior: Carolina Biological/Visuals Unlimited: 19; Corbis: 7 (Roger Ressmeyer), 14 (William Gottlieb), 27 (Firefly Productions); Getty Images: 6 (Photodisc/Ryan McVay), 11 (The Image Bank/Darren Robb); Getty Images/Taxi: 16 (David Ponton), 21 (Carl Schneider), 25 (Robin Lynne Gibson); Getty Images/Taxi/Gabrielle Revere: 13, 15; R. Marguiles/Custom Medical Stock Photo: 9; PhotoEdit: 5 (Bill Aron), 12 (Park Street), 18 (Jonathan Nourok), 23 (Tom McCarthy).

The Child's World®: Mary Berendes, Publishing Director

Editorial Directions, Inc.: E. Russell Primm, Editorial Director; Pam Rosenberg, Editor; Katie Marsico, Associate Editor; Judith Shiffer, Assistant Editor; Matt Messbarger, Editorial Assistant; Susan Hindman, Copy Editor; Sarah E. De Capua, Proofreader; Judith Frisbie, Peter Garnham, Olivia Nellums, Chris Simms, Fact Checkers; Tim Griffin/IndexServ, Indexer; Cian Loughlin O'Day, Photo Researcher; Linda S. Koutris, Photo Editor

The Design Lab: Kathleen Petelinsek, Design; Kari Thornborough, Production Design

Library of Congress Cataloging-in-Publication Data
Gray, Susan Heinrichs.
 The eyes / by Susan H. Gray.
    p. cm. — (The human body)
 Includes index.
  ISBN 1-59296-426-5 (library bound : alk. paper) 1. Eye—Juvenile literature. 2. Vision—Juvenile literature. I. Title.
  QP475.7.G73 2005
  612.8'4—dc22   2005000571

TABLE OF CONTENTS

CHAPTER ONE

AN EARLY MORNING MISTAKE

Tim nearly tripped as he tried to move around in the dark. He was awake before everyone else, so he decided to get dressed for school. He searched through his sock drawer until he found two socks that seemed to match. He slipped them on, put on his shoes, and then went quietly into the kitchen. He fixed a bowl of cereal and sat down to eat.

Soon, his big sister came in. She saw Tim and started laughing. "Who dressed you this morning?" she asked. Tim looked down. He was wearing one red sock and one blue sock. He couldn't figure out how that had happened!

Tim didn't realize that only certain parts of his eyes were able to work in the dark. His eyes saw the socks just fine. But the parts of his

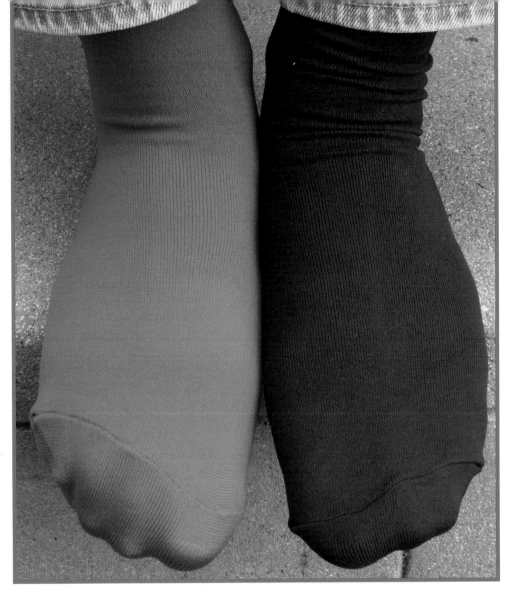

If you get dressed in the dark, you may end up wearing socks of two different colors!

eyes that detected color did not work in the dim light. He had picked

out socks that he thought were the same shade of gray. As he headed

back to his room, Tim reminded himself never to pick out clothes in

the dark again.

CHAPTER TWO

WHAT PARTS MAKE UP THE EYES?

Each eye is a **fluid**-filled ball covered by three layers, or coats, of **tissue.** The outermost layer is the sclera (SKLEHR-uh). We sometimes call this part "the white of the eye."

The sclera is the tough, white, protective outermost coating of the eye.

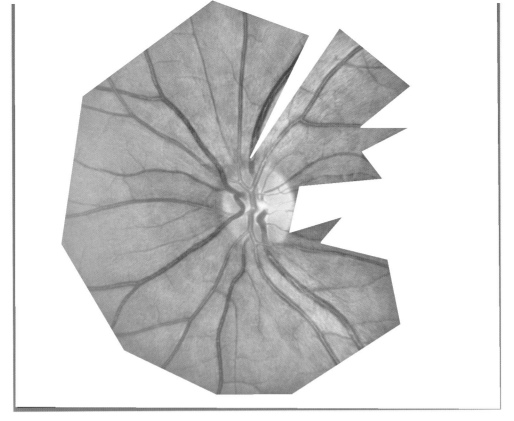

If you could see inside your eye, your retina and optic nerve would look like this.

Just inside the sclera is the choroid (KORE-oyd). It is loaded with

blood vessels. The innermost layer is called the retina (REH-tih-nuh).

This layer is covered with nerve endings that detect light and colors.

At the front of the eye, these three coats are different from the

way they are everywhere else in the eye. Here, the sclera bulges out a

little and is clear instead of white. This clear area is called the cornea

(KORE-nee-uh). The choroid layer is also quite different at the front of the eye. Part of this layer forms the iris—the colored circle of the eye. The iris surrounds a hole called the pupil. It looks like a black spot. Behind the iris is the lens, which helps the eye to focus. The choroid layer has special structures that hold the lens in place. The retina doesn't exist at all in the front of the eye.

Fluid fills all of the space in the eyeball. The area in front of the lens contains a runny, watery fluid. The bulge in the cornea is also filled with this liquid. Behind the lens, the eyeball contains a clear, jellylike fluid. This helps the eyeball to keep its round shape.

A thick stalk comes out of the back of the eye. This stalk contains the optic (OP-tik) nerve, an artery, and a vein. The nerve carries messages about light and color from the retina to the brain. The artery brings oxygen and **nutrients** to the eye tissues. The vein carries away carbon dioxide and waste materials.

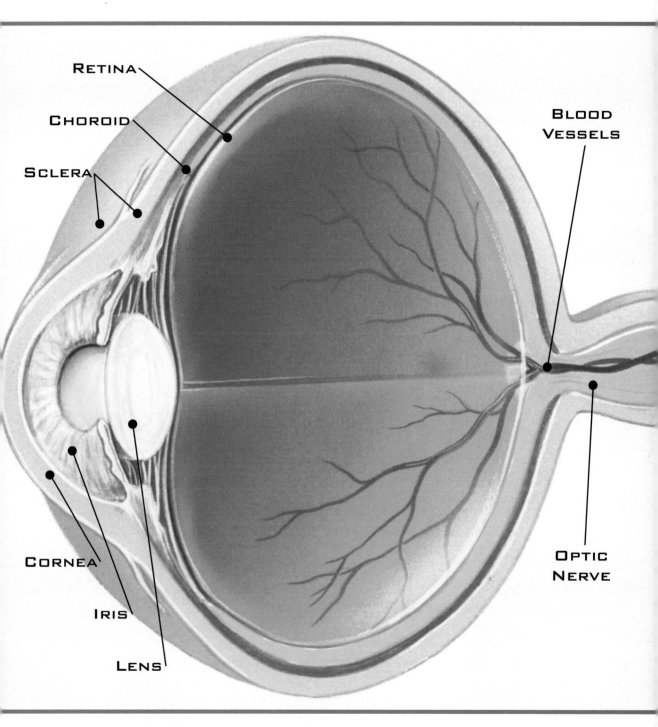

RETINA

CHOROID

SCLERA

BLOOD
VESSELS

CORNEA

IRIS

LENS

OPTIC
NERVE

The different structures that make up the human eye are pictured above.

CHAPTER THREE

WHAT ARE SOME OTHER STRUCTURES AROUND THE EYES?

There are many structures and tissues around the eyes. They protect the eyes and help to move them.

Skull bones almost completely surround the eyes and provide terrific protection. The bony cups holding the eyes are called the orbits. A hole in the back of each orbit allows the optic nerve to pass to the brain. A cushion of fat is packed into the space between the skull bones and the eye.

Six straps of muscle tissue control the movements of each eyeball. The muscles are attached to the eyeball at one end and to orbit bones at the other end. They allow the eyes to roll in every possible direction.

Tear **glands** lie just above the eyes at their outer edges. The glands produce fluid that keeps the eyes moist and washes away dirt. With every blink, the fluid spreads across the eyes.

Each time you blink your eyes you help keep them moist. Blinking also helps wash away any dirt that makes its way into your eye.

Upper and lower eyelids are thin flaps of skin with eyelashes at their edges. By squinting, the eyelids keep out harsh light and dust particles. The eyelashes also help prevent dust from entering the eyes. A very thin, moist **membrane** lines the inside of each eyelid and covers the front of the eye. Sometimes this membrane becomes infected and appears pinkish. A person with an infected membrane is said to have pinkeye.

Eyelashes help keep dirt out of your eyes.

Have you ever noticed that your nose gets runny when you cry? Did you ever wonder why this happens? It has to do with your eyes' drainage system.

Each eye has its own system for producing and draining tears. When you feel sad or hurt, or when your eyes are irritated, a message travels from your brain to your tear glands. The message tells the glands to produce extra fluid. The glands go into action and release this fluid into little tubes called tear ducts. The ducts drain the tears right onto your eyeball. When you cry, these tears wash across your eyes. Some even overflow and run down your face.

The rest of the tears drain through little canals. You can see the openings of these tear canals at the inner corners of the upper and lower eyelids. They look like tiny pinholes. After tears drain into the openings, they travel through the canals and into tear sacs. There are two tear sacs inside the nose—one on the left side and one on the right. The tear sacs open into the nose and drain their extra fluid. This is the fluid that causes your runny nose. Nothing is wrong with your nose—it's just extra tears finding their way out.

CHAPTER FOUR

How Do the Eyes Work?

T o understand how we see things, we first need to understand the retina. The retina contains two kinds of nerve cells that respond to light. These cells are named for their shapes—rods and cones. Rods are very sensitive to light. They help us see things in dim or dark areas. Cones, on the other hand, are sensitive to color and work best in bright light. Rods and cones contain chemicals that break down in the presence of light.

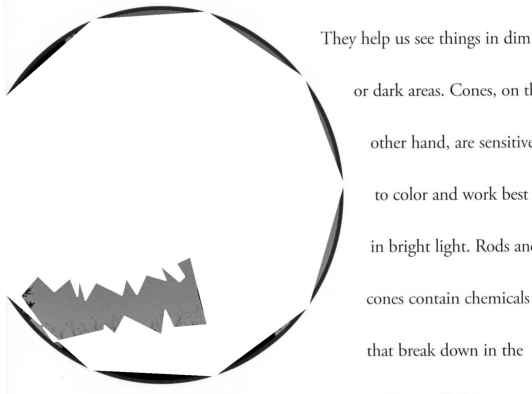

It is hard to see colors in the dark because cone cells work best in bright light.

When light hits an object some colors are absorbed and others are reflected. The walls behind the girl look blue because blue light is being reflected. All the other colors of light are being absorbed.

Light is actually a combination of colors, including red,

yellow, green, and blue. When light hits an object, that object

absorbs some colors and **reflects** others. Objects that

A rainbow is created when sunlight shines through rain, mist, or fog.

appear green are actually reflecting green light. A blue dress

reflects blue light and absorbs the other colors. Rainbows

reveal this combination of colors, called the visible spectrum,

when light shines through drops of water.

Reflected light enters the eye through the pupil. Next,

it passes through the lens and the jellylike fluid and finally

lands on the retina. When light hits the retina's rods and

cones, the chemicals inside them begin to change. The rods

only need a slight amount of light before these chemical

changes begin. The cones' chemicals change when brightly

colored lights hit them. As soon as the chemicals in both

change, messages shoot from the rods and cones through

the optic nerve and to the brain. The brain **interprets**

the messages as pictures.

CHAPTER FIVE

THE FINE TUNING

After light enters the eye and lands on the retina, cells in the retina send signals to the brain. But there's also some fine-tuning that involves the cornea, lens, and iris.

When an image passes through the eye and lands on the retina, it needs to appear sharp and in focus, not blurry. Certain structures in the eye work to make sure this happens. These structures need to bend the incoming light rays.

Your eyes work to bend the light rays coming into them so that the images that form on your retina aren't blurry like this picture.

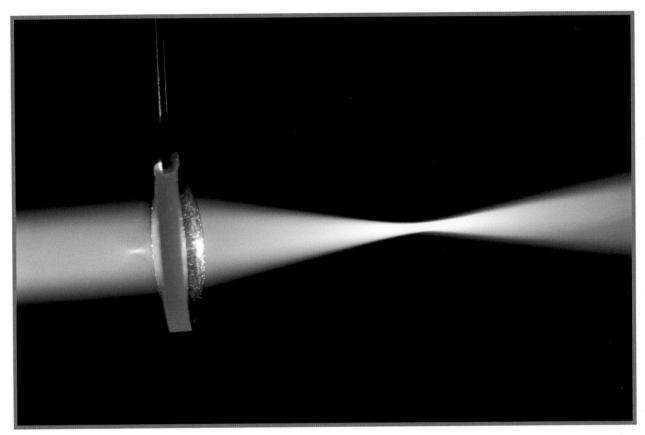

Can you see the point at which the light rays coming through the lens are focused?

Light rays passing through the cornea and lens bend just

enough to form a focused image on the retina. If the image is not

quite focused, the lens works to correct the problem. The structure

holding the lens in place either pulls at the lens to stretch it out

flatter, or it relaxes and allows the lens to become rounded. As the

lens changes shape, it bends the light rays into focus.

You can sometimes notice your own eyes focusing. Try holding up one finger, about 6 inches (15 centimeters) in front of your nose. Don't stare at your finger—focus on something far beyond it. Once you become comfortable viewing the faraway object, suddenly look at your finger. It may take a second or two for you to see your finger clearly. This is because the lenses are changing shape and refocusing.

The colored iris is actually two sets of muscles encircling the pupil. Remember, the pupil is just a hole that lets in light. In a darkened room, one set of iris muscles contracts. The iris draws back and the pupil becomes large so more light can enter. This helps you see in the dark. In bright light, just the opposite happens. The other set of muscles contracts, closing down the pupil to a very small size. This helps you see more clearly and sharply in bright light. The tiny pupil does not allow a lot of extra light to come in and "fog" what you see.

As the ball gets closer and closer to the batter, her eyes must adjust to keep it in focus.

The retina is filled with rods and cones. Scientists say there are about 7 million cones on the retina, and 10 to 20 times as many rods. These cells sense a world of images in front of you, above and below you, and to your sides. But there is one spot on

the retina that can't see a thing. It's at the back of the eye, near where the optic nerve exits. Rods and cones are completely missing, and the area is called the blind spot.

Usually, you don't realize that you have a blind spot. This is because the eyes "cover" for each other. When an image hits the blind spot in one eye, the other eye still sees the image just fine. By closing one eye, however, you can sometimes tell when an image is hitting the blind spot of the other eye.

Try this experiment. Hold this diagram about 20 inches (51 cm) from your face. Cover your left eye, and stare at the round spot with your right eye. Slowly bring the diagram closer, and continue staring at the spot. Without looking directly at it, you will notice that the triangle disappears. At this point, the image of the triangle is landing on your blind spot. The retina is not detecting it at all.

CHAPTER SIX

How Do Glasses Work?

Glasses are extra lenses placed in front of the eyes to help them focus properly. For eyes to focus, they must bend light rays to form a sharp image on the retina. But no matter how hard some people's eyes work, they still can't pull the light rays into focus. The rays form a blurred image on the retina. This is because the retina is either too far back or too far forward to catch the focused image.

In an eyeball that's too long, the retina is too far back. The lens of the eye does its best to pull objects into focus, but it can only do so much. Close-up objects look just fine, but distant objects still appear blurry. People with long eyeballs are said to be nearsighted.

Before eyeglasses were invented, people whose eyes didn't focus properly had to go through life with blurry vision.

In an eyeball that's too short, the retina is much too close to the lens. No matter how hard the lens works to pull objects into focus, it's never perfect. Distant objects appear clear and sharp, but nearby objects seem fuzzy. People with short eyeballs are said to be farsighted.

Usually, glasses can fix these problems. Glasses are made of curved pieces of glass, plastic, or other material that sit directly in front of the eyes. They cause light rays to bend just a tiny bit before they enter the eye. That tiny bend is often enough to help the natural lenses focus the rays clearly onto the retina.

Glasses aren't the only way to help people with poor eyesight. Today, doctors can remove damaged corneas and replace them with healthy ones. They can also replace damaged lenses with artificial models. The eyes are incredible organs,

and doctors are still finding incredible ways to help them do

their work.

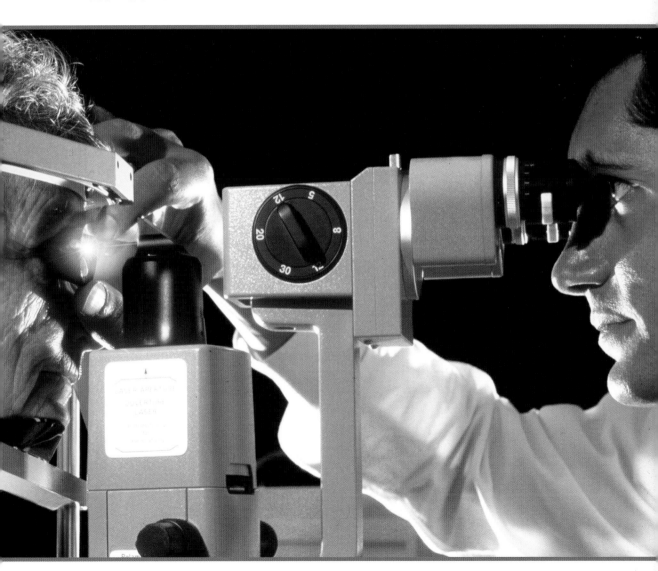

A doctor uses a laser to perform delicate eye surgery.

Glossary

absorbs (ab-ZORBZ) An object that absorbs something soaks it up. When light hits an object, that object absorbs certain colors.

drainage (DRAY-nij) Drainage describes the process of removing fluid from something. When you cry, you might get the sniffles as a result of your eyes' drainage system.

fluid (FLOO-id) A fluid is a substance that flows, such as a liquid. All of the space in the eyeball is filled with fluid.

glands (GLANDZ) Glands are cells or tissues that produce and release fluids. Tear glands produce fluid that keeps the eyes moist and washes away dirt.

interprets (in-TUR-prits) When the brain interprets a signal, it decides what that signal means. When the eye sends messages to the brain, the brain interprets these messages as pictures.

membrane (MEM-brayn) A membrane is a very thin layer that covers other tissues. Membranes line the inside of each eyelid and cover the front of the eye.

nutrients (NOO-tree-uhnts) Nutrients are found in food and are necessary for life and growth. An artery brings oxygen and nutrients to the eye tissues.

reflects (ri-FLEKTS) An object that reflects something throws it back. A blue dress reflects blue light.

tissue (TISH-oo) A tissue is a group of similar cells that make up an organ or body part. The eye is covered by three layers of tissue.

Questions and Answers
about the Eyes

One night, my coach took a picture of our soccer team. In the picture, everyone had red eyes. What happened? Your coach actually photographed the blood vessels in your teammates' eyes! She must have taken a flash photograph because it was dark out. A flash photograph uses a bulb to light up an area as a picture is being taken. In the dim light, everyone's pupils were wide open. When the flash went off, the light entered their big pupils and lit up the blood vessels at the back of their eyes.

Someone told me that if I look cross-eyed, my eyes could get stuck that way. Is this true? When you look cross-eyed, you are forcing your eye muscles to roll both eyes toward your nose. It may feel a little funny, but there's no reason to believe that your eyes will stay that way. Muscles don't just get stuck.

Why do we have eyebrows? Eyebrows protect your eyes from dirt, sweat, and bright sunlight. They also help you express yourself. Lowered eyebrows show that you're angry, while raised eyebrows express surprise.

Did You Know?

- The word *pupil* is taken from the Latin word *pupa,* which means "doll." Long ago, people noticed that when they looked into the pupils of another person, they saw a doll—or a tiny image—of themselves.

- People who are color-blind are missing some of the chemicals in their cones and are therefore unable to see certain colors. Luckily, most color-blind people are missing only one chemical. It is very rare for anyone to be totally color-blind and to see only in black and white.

- Scientists are working hard to develop artificial retinas in which electronic parts detect light and transmit a signal to the optic nerve. This will help restore vision to people who have diseases that have led to blindness.

How to Learn More
about the Eyes

At the Library

Murphy, Patricia J. *Sight*. New York: Children's Press, 2003.

Silverstein, Alvin, Virginia Silverstein, and Laura Silverstein Nunn.
Seeing. Brookfield, Conn.: Twenty-First Century Books, 2001.

Viegas, Jennifer. *The Eye: Learning How We See*.
New York: Rosen Publishing Group, 2002.

On the Web

Visit our home page for lots of links about the eyes:
http://www.childsworld.com/links
Note to Parents, Teachers, and Librarians: We routinely verify our
Web links to make sure they're safe, active sites—so encourage
your readers to check them out!

Through the Mail or by Phone

AMERICAN ACADEMY OF
OPHTHALMOLOGY
PO Box 7424
San Francisco, CA 94120-7424
415/561-8500

NATIONAL FEDERATION OF THE BLIND
1800 Johnson Street
Baltimore, MD 21230
410/659-9314

GLAUCOMA RESEARCH FOUNDATION
490 Post Street, Suite 1427
San Francisco, CA 94102
800/826-6693

Common Eye Disorders

Cataracts (KAT-uh-rakts) are areas of the lens that are cloudy. They often develop in elderly people and in people who work in extremely hot conditions, such as in glassblowing factories. People with cataracts often have a special surgery to help them see better.

A scratched cornea can be quite painful. That is why it is important to be careful to keep objects away from your eyes. If something accidentally gets in your eye and scratches your cornea, you should see your eye doctor right away. He will probably give you eye drops that will help the cornea heal. You might also have to wear a patch over your eye for a day or two. If you do everything your doctor tells you to do, your cornea will be as good as new in just a few days.

Glaucoma (glaw-KO-muh) is a disease in which there is too much watery fluid in front of the lens. This causes pressure to build up in the eye, and it also keeps blood from flowing freely. Without enough blood flowing, some of the nerves in the eye begin to die. Doctors often treat glaucoma with special eye drops.

A detached retina occurs when part of the retina tears away from the tissue beneath it. This sometimes occurs in older people and in those who have had a severe blow to the head. A detached retina sometimes causes blurred eyesight or blindness. Eye doctors can perform surgery to push the retina back into its normal position and seal the tear.

A sty (STYE) is an infection of one of the tiny oil glands at the edge of the eyelid. It usually looks like a small bump. Pressing a warm, damp cloth against the sty can help it open up and drain.

Index

About the Author

Susan H. Gray has a bachelor's and a master's degree in zoology, and has taught college-level anatomy and physiology courses. In her twenty-five years as an author, she has written many medical articles, grant proposals, and children's books. Ms. Gray enjoys gardening, traveling, and playing the piano and organ. She has traveled twice to the Russian Far East to give organ workshops to church musicians. She also works extensively with American and Russian friends to develop medical and social service programs for Vladivostok, Russia. Ms. Gray and her husband, Michael, live in Cabot, Arkansas.